WHAT IS YOUR NAME
LIFE SKILLS
ACTIVITIES

By Terry Perkins

About the book:

These books are user-friendly educational activity books about everyday life skills. They help promote positive decision-making within everyday personal situations. They also open up lines of communication among adolescents, youths, and adults about such topics as secrets, the importance of eating a good breakfast, the Internet, bullying, and peer pressure. The author feels that everyone has a philosophy about life; his philosophy is that teaching is important from an early age. Later on in life there comes a time when we must teach, regardless of our cultural or religious beliefs. Positive change will come in every child's life. This series consists of three volumes. The author believes that to get anywhere in life we have to start somewhere, and home is where we start. Volume #1, *The Apple*, is for age groups four and up. Volume #2, *What is Your Name*, is for age groups eleven and up. Volume #3, *Whose Life is It Anyway*, is for age groups fourteen and up. If we don't teach our children from a young age that it is OK to talk to their parents about their everyday problems, then whom will they talk to? Will they take their questions to the streets, the Internet, or strangers? I hope that they take their questions to you.

This book is intended to help those who may not be able to help themselves.

" Some of the topics in this book should be discussed with a parent or an adult."

Acknowledgments:

With affection and gratitude, I would like to first and foremost acknowledge God. I would also like to thank my mom, Barbara Jean, as well as my brother, my sisters, my sons, my nieces, and my nephews: Ethen, Taniya, Tiara, Tracy Jr., London, Bryan, Brittney, Brandon, Denarco, Maurice, Travis, Tayja, Tyshaw. I would also like to acknowledge my aunt Marva, Raymond, my cousins, and all of my family and friends—near and far, young and old, living and deceased. I love you all. We can always learn from each other no matter what. Sharing is caring and love has no boundaries. The only limitations you have are the limitations that you place on yourself. I try to learn from everyone who crosses my path and everything that crosses my path in life. There are no mistakes; there are only opportunities. Excuses become things of the past once you know right from wrong.

Table of Contents

Let's Talk About
FAMILY

Do you have a big family?

Are you an only child?

Do you get along with everybody in your family?

Do members of your family fight often?

Whom in your family don't you get along with?

Whom in your family do you get along with the best?

Besides your mother and your father, whom in your family would you like to live with?

Do you wish you had a brother or a sister?

Date   /   /

Let's Talk About
YOUR NAME

Are you named after anyone in your family?

Do you know the meaning of your name?

Do you like your name?

Do other kids make fun of your name?

Do you want to change your name?

Do you use a nickname because you don't like your real name?

Do you like the sound of your name?

Do you wish your name was someone else name?

Date   /   /

Let's Talk About
TAKING RISK

Do you take risks because your friends dare you to?

Do you take risks because you think no one cares about you?

Do you take risks because you want attention?

Do you take risks to fit in with your friends?

Do you take risks because you want to hurt yourself?

Do you take risks because you're mad at someone?

Do you take risks because someone told you it was cool?

Date   /   /

Let's Talk About
RESPONSIBILITY

What does responsibility mean to you?

Do you think you will be able to handle some responsibilities when you get older?

Do your friends think you are a responsible person?

Do your mom and dad trust that you are responsible when you are away from home?

Do your brother and sister trust you to be responsible with their things?

Do you let your friends break your things?

When you come home from school, do you throw your clothes on the floor or do you hang them up?

Date   /   /

Let's Talk About
BEING HOME ALONE

What do you do when you are at home alone?

Do you clean up the house when you are home alone?

Do you make the house messy when you are home alone?

Do you invite your friends over when you are home alone?

Do you do your homework when you are home alone?

Do you hang out in front of your home when you are home alone?

Do you cry when you are home alone?

Date   /   /

Let's Talk About
RACISM

What does racism to you?

Do you know where racism comes from?

Do you know how you can stop racism?

Have you ever witnessed racism?

Do you think that you can be racist toward a person of the same race as you?

Do you think that people are born racist?

Would you like to help abolish racism?

Do you think that you help spread racism?

Date   /   /

Let's Talk About
SKIPPING SCHOOL

Have you ever wanted to skip school because someone was threatening you?

Have you ever wanted to skip school because your friends were skipping school?

Have you ever wanted to skip school because you were failing in some of your classes?

Have you ever wanted to skip school because you were ashamed of the way you are dressed?

Have you ever wanted to skip school because you felt you were not as smart as the other students?

Have you ever wanted to skip school because someone hurt you at home?

Date / /

Let's Talk About
RIDING THE SCHOOL BUS

How are you supposed to act on the school bus?

Are you supposed to stand up while the bus is moving?

Are you supposed to holler out the window?

Are you supposed to talk back to the bus driver?

Are you supposed to throw things out the window?

Are you supposed to fight on the school bus?

Are you supposed to make a lot of noise on the school bus?

Date   /   /

Let's Talk About
MANNERS

Who can you learn good manners from?

Do you think that you should use good manners all the time or only some of the time?

What cartoons on TV can you learn good manners from?

Do you think adults should have good manners too?

Do you think that you only need to have good manners when you are at home?

Do you think that you need to have good manners when you are out with your friends?

Do you think that other kids should use good manners too?

Date   /   /

Let's Talk About
HABITS

What does the word *habit* mean to you?

What kind of habits do you have?

What bad habits do you have?

What good habits do you have?

Do you know that you can change your bad habits into good habits?

Whom do you think you can learn good habits from?

Do your mom and dad teach you to have good habits or bad habits?

Date   /   /

Let's Talk About
MONEY

How do you think you can earn money?

Do you know how to count money?

Do you know how to count your change when you are at the store?

Can you add up coins and dollars together?

If you don't know how to count, who can help you learn to count?

Do you save the money earn or do you spend it all?

Do you give your money to other kids?

Have you ever lost your moms money on the way to the store?

Date   /   /

Let's Talk About
GIRL FRIENDS

Who are your new girl friends?

If you are a girl, do you have a girl friend?

Where do your new girl friends live?

Do your girl friends ever come over to your house?

Do you ever go over to your girl friend's house?

What is your new girl friend's nationality?

Do you and your girl friends hang out together at school?

Where do you and your girl friends spend your time?

Do you like hanging out with your girl friends instead of
your guy friends?

Are all of your girl friends quiet?

Do you and your girl friends like to do the same things?

What kinds of hairstyles do your girl friends have?

Are some of your girl friends troublemakers?

Do some of your girl friends like talking about other people's business?

Do some of your girl friends smoke cigarettes?

Do some of your girl friends do drugs?

Date   /   /

Let's Talk About
GUY FRIENDS

Who are your guy friends?

Do any of your guy friends belong to any gangs?

Do you and your guy friends hang out at your house?

If you are not hanging out at your home, where do you and your guy friends hang out?

Do any of your guy friends play sports?

Are any of your male friends a member of a singing group?

Whom do you hang out with at school?

Are some of your guy friends in some of the same classes?

Date   /   /

Let's Talk About
CHOICES

Do you know how to make good choices?

Has anyone ever told you to do something that is the wrong choice to you?

What happens when you make a bad choice?

Have you ever made a bad choice before?

Do you ever think you will run out of choices to make?

In what situation would you not have a choice to make?

Date   /   /

Let's Talk About
LYING

Do you like to tell lies?

Do you tell lies to get others in trouble?

Do you tell lies because your friends have told you to lie?

Do you tell lies for your friends?

Do you tell lies because you think it's cool?

Do you tell lies when you think you will get into trouble if you tell the truth?

Do you tell lies after you do something that your mom or dad told you not to do?

Date   /   /

Let's Talk About
NEW ASSOCIATES

Do you know what an associate is?

Would you consider an associate to be a friend?

Do your new associates like to steal?

Do your new associates like to experiment with drugs?

Do your new associates like to smoke cigarettes?

Do your new associates like getting into trouble all the time?

Do your new associates like to play sports?

Date   /   /

Let's Talk About
YOUR SURROUNDINGS

Do you know what your surroundings are?

Do you pay attention to what's going on around you when you are away from home?

Do you like the surroundings where you live?

Do you like your surroundings at school?

Are the surroundings safe where you play?

Are the surroundings where you play clean?

Do you think that the surroundings where you live are safe at night?

Date   /   /

Let's Talk About
CLOTHES

What kinds of clothes do you like to wear?

Do you think that your clothes make you who you are?

Do you think that the clothes you wear make other kids respect you more?

Do you let your friends wear your clothes?

Who pays for the clothes you wear?

Do you hang up your clothes or throw them onto the floor?

Do you wish that you had nicer clothes?

Date   /   /

Let's Talk About
CYBERBULLYING

What is cyberbullying?

Have you ever used a computer to threaten anyone?

Have you ever used a computer to say bad things about anybody?

Have you and your friends ever used a computer to threaten anyone?

Have you ever used a computer to spread lies about anyone?

Do you use your computer to put pictures of your friends on the Internet without his or her permission?

Do you use your computer to start rumors about people that you used to date?

Date   /   /

Let's Talk About
GETTING CAUGHT UP

What does "getting caught up" mean to you?

How do you avoid getting caught up?

Who can you go to if you get caught up in some trouble?
Why?

Do you do things that you have been told not to do? Why?

Do you go to places that you have been told not to go?
Why?

Do you think that you are always supposed to do what
your friends are doing?

Do you think that your friends care if you get into trouble
or not?

If you get caught up in some trouble, whose fault do you
think it is? Why?

Date   /   /

Let's Talk About
FAIRNESS

Do you think that life is fair? Why or why not?

Do you think that people should give you what you want?

Do you think that people should steal things from other people just because their family can't afford to buy them?

Do you think that people should be mean to other people because they are mad at them?

Do you think that people should do whatever they want to do to you just because they are bigger than you?

Do you think that everybody should be treated the same?

Do you think that some people have it better because of the color of their skin?

Date   /   /

Let's Talk About
POSSIBLITIES

Do you know what your possibilities are?

Do you think that your possibilities are limited by where you live?

Do you think that your possibilities are limited by the color of your skin?

Do you think that the school that you go to limits your possibilities?

Do you think that your possibilities are limited because of your family?

Do you think that your possibilities are limited because of your friends?

Date   /   /

Let's Talk About
HARDHEADEDNESS

Do you think that you are hardheaded?

Do people have to keep telling you over and over again not to do something?

Do you always get into trouble because you are always doing what you are not supposed to be doing?

Do you think that you are hardheaded?

Do you always do what people tell you to do?

Do you always do what your friends tell you to do?

Do you always do things that your mom and dad have told you not to do?

Date   /   /

Let's Talk About
RIGHT AND WRONG

How do you know right from wrong?

How do you feel when you are doing something wrong?

How do you feel when you want to do the right thing but your friends want you to do the wrong thing?

How do you feel when you are telling the truth but no one believes you?

How do you feel when you are not sure about what to do?

Is doing the right thing positive or negative?

Is doing the right thing confusing sometimes?

Date   /   /

Let's Talk About
HAVING BABIES

At what age do you think it is appropriate to have a baby?

Do you want to have a baby? Why?

Do any of your friends want to have a baby?

Are you having unprotected sex? Why?

Are you trying to get pregnant? Why?

Do you think you might be pregnant?

Do you think that you should have a baby because you are in love?

Where would you and your baby live?

Who would help you take care of your baby?

Who will watch your baby while you are in school?

Who will take your baby to the hospital when you are unable to take it?

Who will buy clothes for your baby?

Who will buy diapers for your baby when you are unable to buy them?

Who will take care of your baby when you get sick?

Date   /   /

Let's Talk About
EXCUSES

Do you always have an excuse for the things you do?

Do you tell other kids what to say when they are in trouble?

Do you think that you can talk your way out of anything? Why?

Do you think that you are smarter than your mother and your father?

Do you feel like nobody can tell you anything? Why?

Do you always get caught telling lies? Why?

Do your friends tell you that you think you know everything?

Date   /   /

Let's Talk About
THE WRONG PLACE AT THE WRONG TIME

Do you know what it means to be in the wrong place at the wrong time?

Have you ever been in the wrong place at the wrong time?

Have you ever been somewhere at the wrong time and gotten blamed for something that you did not do?

Do you go to places that you are not supposed to go to?

Do you go to places where you might get into trouble?

Do you go to places with your friends that you are not supposed to go to?

Date   /   /

Let's Talk About
WALKING TO SCHOOL

Do you get into trouble on your way to school?

Do your friends try to get you to do bad things when you are walking to school?

Does walking to school make you late for school?

Do you ever get to take the bus to school?

Do you walk to school with the same friends every day?

Do you walk to school because you are afraid to take the bus?

Have you ever been kicked off of the school bus?

Date   /   /

Let's Talk About
WALKING HOME FROM SCHOOL

If you are not allowed to ride the bus home, whom do you walk home with?

Do you walk home with the same friends every day?

Do you walk home from school because you got kicked off of the bus for misbehaving?

Has someone told you not to get on the school bus?

Does your mom or your dad know that you are walking home from school?

Have you told anyone in your family that you are walking home from school?

Date   /   /

Let's Talk About
PUBLIC TRANSPORTATION

Have you ever taken public transportation to school?

Whom do you catch the bus with in the morning?

What bus route do you take to get to school?

At what time do you have to get up to catch the bus and not be late for school?

Do you have to take more than one bus to get to school?

Is it ever dark outside when you go to catch your bus in the morning?

Do you and your friends talk about people on the bus?

Date   /   /

Let's Talk About
HITCHHIKING

Do you know what hitchhiking is?

Have you ever tried to hitchhike to get home from school?

Do you think that it is safe for you to hitchhike to get home from school or to go to school?

Do your friends ever try to get you to hitchhike to get home from school?

Do strangers ever try to pick you up or talk to you when you are walking home from school?

Date   /   /

Let's Talk About
MISSING THE SCHOOL BUS

What do you do when you miss the school bus?

Do you think that you will get in trouble if you miss the school bus?

Have you ever missed the school bus on purpose?

Have you ever missed the school bus because you like to walk home?

Have you ever missed the school bus so that you could hang out with your friends?

Date   /   /

Let's Talk About
COMMUNICATION

How do you communicate with others?

How many different ways can you communicate with people when you are in trouble?

Can you communicate with someone without talking?

Can you communicate with someone by writing a letter to him or her?

Can you communicate with someone by leaving a message with him or her?

Can you communicate with someone by using sign language?

How can you communicate with someone to let him or her know that you are in trouble and you need help?

Date   /   /

Let's Talk About
BRAGGING

Do you brag about the things that you have? Why?

Do you make fun of people because they don't have the things you have? Why?

Do you think that it is OK to feel better than other people just because you have nice things? Why?

Do your mom and dad like it when you act like you are better than other people?

Do you brag to show off for your friends?

Do you brag to show off for girls or boys?

Do you brag because you don't feel important?

Date   / /

Let's Talk About
PARTIES

Do you go to parties on the weekend?

At your age, are you too young to go to parties?

Do you want to go to parties even though you are not allowed to?

Were you ever not allowed to go to a party because you had been bad?

How do you act at parties?

Do you dance when you go to parties?

Do you simply sit around and look at the other kids having fun?

Do they have games for you to play when you are at parties?

Date   /   /

Let's Talk About
GOALS

Can you tell me what a goal is?

When do you think you should start working toward your goals?

Do you think that your goals have to be big?

Do you know what a short-term goal is?

Do you know what a long-term goal is?

Do you think that you can change your goals?

Do you think that you can have more than one goal at a time?

Who do you think can help you with your goals?

Date   /   /

Let's Talk About
YOUR NEEDS

What do you think you need to make you happy? Why?

Do you think that you need food? Why?

Do you think that you need a home to live in? Why?

Do you need clothes to wear? Why?

Do you think that you need to wear shoes? Why?

Do you think that you need clean water to drink? Why?

Do you think that you need money? Why?

Date   /   /

Let's Talk About
YOUR WANTS

Do you think your wants are more important than your needs?

Do you want to have a new car? Why?

Do you want to have a big house? Why?

Do you want to have a lot of money? Why?

Do you want to have nice clothes? Why?

Do you want to have a lot of jewelry? Why?

Do you want to marry a rich boyfriend or girlfriend? Why?

Date   /   /

Let's Talk About
PERSONALTIES

Do you know what *personality* means?

Do you know what kind of personality you have?

Does your mom, your dad, or another family member have a personality that is similar to yours?

Whom do people say that you are similar to?

Do you think that your personality can change?

Do you want to change your personality?

Do people say that you have a nice personality or a bad one?

Date   /   /

Let's Talk About
MAKING MISTAKES

Do you think that you are perfect?

Do you think that we all make mistakes?

How do you feel when you make a mistake?

Are you afraid to try new things because you worry that you might make a mistake?

Do you think that someone will get mad at you for making mistakes?

Do you think that you will get yelled at if you make a mistake?

Did you know that making mistakes is OK as long as you don't continue to make the same mistakes?

Date   /   /

Let's Talk About
BEING ON TIME

Who benefits from being on time?

Do you have trouble being on time? Why?

Do you think that everyone should wait for you?

Do you care about whether or not you are on time?

Has anyone ever told you that it is OK to show up whenever you want to?

Do you have trouble showing up on time because you are high all the time?

Are you regularly late because you don't know how to tell time?

Date   /   /

Let's Talk About
PERSONAL PROBLEMS

What do you think a personal problem is?

How do you deal with your personal problems at school?

Who can help you with your personal problems?

Do you try to solve your problems by doing nothing and simply hoping that they will go away?

Do you try to handle your personal problems by yourself?

Do you have trouble trusting other people with your personal problems? Why?

Do you run and hide when you have personal problems? Why?

Date   /   /

Let's Talk About
APOLOGIZING

Do you know what the word *apology* means?

Have you ever apologized to someone when you knew that you had done something wrong?

Have you ever apologized to someone for saying something that was not nice?

Have you ever apologized for breaking something that was your friend's?

Have you ever apologized for hurting someone's feelings?

Have you ever apologized for taking something that didn't belong to you?

Date   /   /

Let's Talk About
CHORES

Do you help out with chores around the house?

Do like doing chores?

What chore do you hate the most? Why?

Do you ever forget to do your chores and then just go to bed?

Do you ever pay someone else to do your chores for you?

Do you feel that you should get paid for helping out around the house? Why?

Is keeping your room clean one of your chores?

Date   /   /

Let's Talk About
EATING

Do you like to eat all the time?

What do you like to eat? Why?

Do think that you should be on a diet? Why?

Do you think that you will get sick if you eat? Why?

Do you think that you are overweight? Do you know why you are overweight?

Do you only eat once a day because you think that you are fat?

Do you eat and then throw up? Why?

Do you throw your food in the garbage?

Do you wear a lot of clothes to hide your weight?

Date   /   /

Let's Talk About
PERSONAL HYGIENE

Do you know what personal hygiene is?

Do you think that you should take baths every day?

Do you try to brush your teeth three times a day?

Do you wash your hands before you eat?

Do you wash your hands after you go to the bathroom?

Do you like wearing deodorant?

Do you put on clean underwear every day?

Date   /   /

Let's Talk About
BEDTIME

At what time do you go to bed at night?

Do you go to bed whenever you want to?

Do you take a nap when you come home from school?

Do you have to be in bed at a certain time?

Do you take a bath before you go to bed at night or do you take a bath in the morning?

Do you have to do any chores before you go to bed?

Do you think that you can get up for school on time when you go to bed whenever you want to?

Date   /   /

Let's Talk About
LATE NIGHTS

Are you out late at night? Why?

Do you come home whenever you want to? Why?

Do you stay out late because your friends stay out late?

Do you like being out at night because you have more fun at night?

Do you go out at night when there are no adults at home?

Are you always late for school? Why?

Do you always fall asleep in class? Why?

Date   /   /

Let's Talk About

DECISIONS

Do you think that you are a good decision-maker?

Do you help others make decisions?

Who can help you make the right decision?

When was the last time that you had to make a decision?

When do you need an adult to help you make decisions?

Do you think that you should make all of your decisions on your own?

Date   /   /

Let's Talk About
ENEMIES

Who are your enemies?

Why do you think people have enemies?

Do you think that you have enemies because of where you live?

Do you think that you have enemies because of the clothes you wear?

Do you think that you have enemies because of your friends?

Do you think that you have enemies because of the things you own?

Do you think that you have enemies because of your boyfriend or girlfriend?

Date   /   /

Let's Talk About
OUR HANDS

Why do we have to keep our hands to ourselves?

Are boys supposed to put their hands on girls?

Are girls supposed to put their hands on boys?

Are boys and girls supposed to touch each other?

Are adults supposed to put their hands on kids?

Are kids supposed to hit on adults?

If someone hits on you, what are you supposed to do?

Date   /   /

Let's Talk About
ENVY

Do you know what the word *envy* means?

Why do people envy what other people have?

Do you envy anyone because of the things that they have?

Does it make you feel angry when people have nicer things than you?

Date   /   /

Let's Talk About
PHYSICAL DISABILITES

Do you have any physical disabilities?

Do you know what it means to have a physical disability?

How do you think you are supposed to treat someone with a physical disability?

Do you think that people with physical disabilities know when you are making fun of them?

Do you think that they will ever need your help?

Date   /   /

Let's Talk About
FUN

Where do you have the most fun?

What are some fun things you do?

Do you have fun at home?

Do you have more fun at your friends' houses?

Are you allowed to play at your home?

Do you have to go outside to play?

What fun games do you like to play at home?

What fun games do you like to play at school?

Date   /   /

Let's Talk About

TAKING TEST

Do you have trouble taking tests?

Do you study before you take a test?

Who helps you study for your tests?

How do you feel before a test?

Do you think that you should get plenty of rest the night before you take a test?

Do you think that you will do better on your tests if you eat a good breakfast?

What do you think is the hardest part of taking a test?

Date   /   /

Let's Talk About
MEMORY

How good do you think your memory is?

Do you have trouble memorizing certain things?

Are you good at memorizing numbers?

Are you good at memorizing names?

Are you good at memorizing faces?

Are you good at memorizing directions?

Are you good at memorizing how to spell words?

Are good at good at memorizing puzzles pieces?

Date   / /

Play a memory game:

Do this exercise with a parent or an adult.

Date   /   /

Let's Talk About
RULES

Do this exercise with a parent or an adult.

What does the word *rule* mean to you?

What rules do you dislike? Why?

Do you have any rules at your home?

Do you have any rules at your school?

Do you want to make up your own set of rules?

Do you think that some rules are good?

Do you think that you need to follow the rules?

Why don't you think that you should have to follow any of the rules?

Date   /   /

Let's Talk About
ADVICE

Do you know what the word *advice* means?

Who do you ask for advice?

Do you think that all advice is good advice?

What kind of advice do your friends give you?

Do you think that anyone has ever given you bad advice before?

How can you tell if someone has given you bad advice or good advice?

Do you think that good advice will get you into trouble?

Date   /   /

Let's Talk About
THE BLAME GAME

Do you blame all of the bad things that happen to you on other people?

When you get in trouble, is it ever someone else's fault?

When you get bad grades in school, is it ever someone else's fault?

When you choose to do drugs or to not do drugs, is it ever someone else's fault?

Do you do things without thinking about what you are doing?

Do you blame your mom and dad for all of the problems that you have in your life?

Date   /   /

Let's Talk About
THE BEST PART OF YOUR DAY

What was the best part of your day?

Do you like the morning time?

Do you like the afternoon?

Do you like the evening?

Do you like the nighttime?

Do you like going to school every day?

Do you like going to the mall with your friends?

Date   /   /

Let's Talk About
DOING YOUR BEST

Do you feel good when you know that you have done your best?

Who do you think benefits when you do your best? Why?

Do you think that people will laugh at you when you try to do your best?

Do your friends think that you are trying to be better than them whenever you do your best?

Do you think that your friends are holding you back from doing your best? Why?

Do you think that your height and weight have anything to do with your ability to do your best?

Do you think that your ability to do your best is affected by where you live? Why?

Date   /   /

Let's Talk About
BEHAVIOR

How good is your behavior?

Do you feel that you are always on your best behavior?

Do you think that your behavior accurately expresses the way that you feel?

Do you think that your behavior changes depending on where you are?

Do you think that your behavior changes depending on whom you are with?

Do you think that you should improve your behavior?

Do you think that your behavior gets you into trouble?

Date   /   /

Let's Talk About
NAME-CALLING

Do you like to call other people bad names?

How does it feel when someone calls you bad names?

How do you think it makes other people feel when you call them bad names?

Do you like it when someone calls your sister or your brother bad names?

Do you like it when someone calls your mother or your father bad names?

How do you deal with people calling you bad names?

Do you start crying when someone calls you bad names?

Date   /   /

Let's Talk About

GETTING INTO TROUBLE

Do you always get into trouble with the same friends? Why?

Do you hang out where you're not supposed to hang out?

Do you listen to your mom and dad when they tell you not to hang out with certain friends?

Do you get into trouble just to get attention?

Do you get into trouble so that people will think that you are tough?

Do you get into trouble because you have a drug problem?

Do you get into trouble because you want to fit in with your new friends?

Date   /   /

Let's Talk About
LOSS OF INTEREST

Do you know what it means to lose interest in something?

When do you think you start losing interest in things? Why?

What do you do when you start losing interest in something?

What things do you find interesting? Why?

How can you make things more interesting for yourself?

When things are easy for you, do you lose interest more quickly? Why?

When you can't do things your own way, do you lose interest in what you are doing? Why?

Date   /   /

Let's Talk About
ATTITUDE

What kind of attitude do you have?

Do you think that you have a good attitude?

What do your friends think about your attitude?

What do your teachers think about your attitude?

What do your parents think about your attitude?

Do you think that your attitude accurately expresses the way that you feel?

Do you think that your attitude has resulted from your environment?

Date   /   /

Let's Talk About
EDUCATION

What does the word *education* mean to you?

Why do you think you need a good education?

Where do you think you can get the best education?

Do you think that being more educated makes you smarter?

Do you think that education is supposed to get easier from one grade to the next?

Do you think that having a good education will help you get a better job?

Do you think that having a good education will give you more career opportunities?

Date   /   /

Let's Talk About
WHAT YOU LIKE ABOUT
YOUR NEW SCHOOL

1

2

3

4

Date   /   /

Let's Talk About
WHAT YOU DON'T LIKE
ABOUT YOUR NEW SCHOOL

Do this exercise with a parent or an adult.

1

2

3

4

Date   /   /

Let's Talk About
YOUR CLASSES

What is your favorite class?

How many classes do you have?

Do you feel that you have too many classes?

Do you think that you need some help with some of your classes?

Do you get along with all your classmates?

Do some of your classes seem to be harder than others?

Do you feel that you are failing in some of your classes?

Do you get along with all of your teachers in all of your classes?

Do you feel that your teacher is giving you too much to do?

Do you think that some of your classes are too hard?

Do you think that some of your classes are too easy?

Do you think that some of your teachers are moving too quickly for you?

Are you bored with some of your classes?

Do you fall asleep in any of your classes?

Do you play around in some of your classes?

Do you have trouble finding all of your classes?

Date   /   /

Let's Talk About
FACT OR FICTION

Do this exercise with a parent or an adult.

Answer the following questions with the word *fact* or *fiction*.

You can be anything that you want to be in life.

Selling drugs is the only way to make money.

The color of your skin determines what you can accomplish in life.

The kinds of clothes you wear make you better than other people.

The location of your home makes you better than other people.

Everything in life should be free.

Everyone is going to let you have your way all the time.

Date   /   /

Let's Talk About
SCHOOL SUBJECTS

What is your favorite subject at school? Why?

What subject at school is the hardest for you? Why?

Do you have trouble understanding certain subjects? Why?

Do you get along with all of your teachers at school?

Do you think that some of your teachers need to spend more time with you in some of your classes?

Are problems at your home making it hard for you to study?

Why do you think that some subjects are harder for you to understand?

Date   /   /

Let's Talk About
TALENTS

Do you think that you don't have any talents?

What talents do you think you were born with?

Do you think that other people are more talented than you?

Do you think that you have to work harder than others?

Do you think that you have to accept things that other people give you?

Are you afraid that people will laugh at you because of the way you sing or dance?

Do you think that you can only have one talent?

Do you think that you always have to settle for second best?

Date   /   /

Let's Talk About
STRIVING

What does the word _striving_ mean to you?

Are you currently striving toward any goals?

Have you ever strived for anything in the past?

Can you think of anything that you would like to strive for in the near future?

How do you plan to accomplish anything I life if you don't strive for it?

Do you think that striving means to give up or to try harder?

Are you able to ask anyone to help you with the things that you would like to strive for?

Date   /   /

THINK

ABOUT WHAT

YOU WOULD LIKE TO DO

AND

GO

FOR

IT.

Let's Talk About
TELLING TIME

Do you know how to tell time?

Do you feel that you don't need to know how to tell time?

Do you know what military time is?

Do you know what the four different time zones are?

Do you know how to set a watch?

Do you know how to set an alarm clock?

Do you know the difference between a.m. and p.m.?

Date   /   /

Let's Talk About
INTERPERSONAL SKILLS

Do you know what interpersonal skills are?

What do you like to do?

Do you like sports?

Do you like working with animals?

**Do you like working with kids who are younger than you
are?**

Do you like helping people?

Do you like taking orders?

Do you like acting?

Date   /   /

Let's Talk About
SPELLING

Do you need people to help you spell words?

Do you worry that people will laugh at you if you ask for help with your spelling?

Do you think that your ability to spell affects your ability to read?

Do you think that you can read without knowing how to spell?

Do you like taking spelling tests?

Which words are hard for you to spell? Why?

Do you have trouble pronouncing certain words?

Date   /   /

Let's Talk About
READING

Do you have trouble reading?

Do you have trouble putting words together?

Do you need help to improve your ability to read?

Do you think that you have a speech problem? Why?

Do you think that your friends will make fun of you if they know that you need help to improve your ability to read?

Which words are the hardest for you to learn?

Do you like reading out loud?

What is the hardest part about reading?

Date   /   /

Let's Talk About
MATH

Do you need help to improve your ability to do math?

Do you think that some math problems are too hard for you?

Do you feel that the teacher is going too fast for you sometimes?

Do you feel that you would catch on more quickly if you had more time?

Do you feel that you need extra help?

Do you know what a tutor is?

Do you think that you could get along without math?

Date   /   /

Let's Talk About

HISTORY

Do you like history?

Do you think that history gives you a better understanding of your heritage?

Do you think that history is important for you? Why?

Do you think that you will have the chance to make history?

Who is your favorite historian? Why?

What do you like the most about history?

Do you think that history is the only thing that we should study? Why?

Date   /   /

Let's Talk About
SCIENCE

Do you like science? Why?

Do you think that science is interesting?

Would you want to become a scientist someday?

Do you like studying things?

Do you like inventing things?

Date   /   /

Let's Talk About
EXERCISING

Do you like taking care of yourself?

Do you like walking?

Do you like running?

Do you like swimming?

Do you like lifting weights?

Do you like doing aerobics?

Do you like playing sports?

Date   /   /

Let's Talk About
FRIUT

Do you think that fruit is good for you? Why?

How many times a day should you eat fruit?

Do you think that fruit is healthy?

Do you think that you could live solely off of fruit?

What kinds of fruit do you like to eat?

What kinds of fruit do you not like to eat?

What meals can you make with fruit?

What meals can you add fruit too?

Date   /   /

Let's Talk About
VEGTABLES

Are fruits and vegetables the same?

What is the difference between fruits and vegetables?

Where can you find vegetables?

Of fruits and vegetables, which is better for you?

Can you find the same vitamins in fruits that you do in vegetables?

Do fruits and vegetables grow the same way?

What fruits and vegetables grow year round?

Why do you think some animals eat only fruits and vegetables?

Date   /   /

Let's Talk About
PHYSICAL EDUCATION

Do you like physical education? Why or why not?

What grades do you get in your physical education class?

What topics do you discuss in class?

Do you dress every day for class?

Do they teach you about sports?

Do they teach you sex education?

Do they teach you how to swim?

Date   /   /

Let's Talk About
AFTER-SCHOOL PROGRAMS

What after-school programs are you involved in?

Do you like to play sports?

Do you like to swim?

Does your school have a drill team?

Are you a cheerleader for your school's basketball team?

Do you do any tutoring after school?

Are you a member of your school's band?

Date   /   /

Let's Talk About
WHAT YOU WANT TO BE
WHEN YOU GROW UP
Do this exercise with a parent or an adult.

1.

2.

3.

Date   /   /

Let's Talk About
GROWING UP

What does growing up mean to you?

Do you think that you will make better choices when you are grown up?

Do you think that your parents will trust you more when you are grown up?

Do you think that you should stop acting like a child when you are grown up?

Do you think that you should take better care of your possessions when you are grown up?

Do you think that you should clean up after yourself when you are grown up?

Date   /   /

Let's Talk About
MINDSET

Do you know what the word *mindset* means?

Do you like saving every penny you get?

Do you know what a positive mindset is?

Did you know that your mindset helps you deal with daily life?

Did you know that your mindset affects the choices that you make?

Do you think that you are a selfish person or a generous person?

Do you like thinking positively or negatively?

Date /   /

Let's Talk About
CREATIVITY

How do you express your creativity?

Do you like building things? Why?

Do you like cooking? Why?

Do you like singing? Why?

Do you like doing modern dance? Why?

Do you like acting on the stage? Why?

Do you like composing music? Why?

Date   /   /

Let's Talk About
THE DAYS OF THE WEEK

What are the days of the week?

1.

2.

3.

4.

5.

6.

7.

Date   /   /

Let's Talk About

THE MONTHS OF THE YEAR

What are the months of the year?

1.

2.

3.

4.

5.

6.

7.

8.

9.

10.

11.

12.

Date   /   /

Let's Talk About
MUSIC

What kind of music do you like to listen to? Why?

Do you listen to music before you go to school?

Do you listen to music when you get home from school?

Do you listen to music before you go to bed?

Do you watch music videos all day?

Do you believe everything that you see in music videos? Why?

Do you want to be like the people in the music videos? Why?

Date   /   /

Let's Talk About
CONFUSION

Do you know what the word *confusion* mean?

Have you ever been confused about anything?

Do you think that it is OK to feel confused?

Do you think that it is normal to always feel confused?

Do your friends try to confuse you sometimes?

When you are confused about something, do you feel that you have to spend more time than other people thinking about it?

When an activity is confusing, do you stop doing it or do you try to figure it out on your own?

Date   /   /

Let's Talk About
PEER PRESSURE

What does the phrase *peer pressure* mean to you?

How do you feel about peer pressure?

How can you deal with peer pressure?

Do you think that everybody deals with peer pressure in the same way?

Do you think that some peer pressure can be good?

Whom should you go to when peer pressure becomes too hard to handle?

Have you ever tried to pressure any of your peers?

Date   /   /

Let's Talk About
COMPUTERS

Do you know how many parts are in a typical computer?

Do you know the names of all of the different computer parts?

Do you have a computer at home?

Do you like playing with computers?

Would you like to get a job working with computers?

Would you like to show someone how computers work?

Are you able to teach people how to use computers?

Date   /   /

Let's Talk About
PLAYING

Where do you have the most fun?

How long are you allowed to play outside each day?

Do you have a curfew?

Are you allowed to go to the playground in your neighborhood?

Who takes you to the playground?

Do you have to stay in front of your house and play?

Is your neighborhood too dangerous for you to play outside?

If you can't play outside, what do you do instead?

What kinds of games do you play with your friends?

Date   /   /

Let's Talk About
PATIENCE

Do you feel that everything should happen when you want it to happen?

When you wait for something to happen, does it seem like it will never happen?

Do you think that everything happens in its own given time?

Do you think that the world was made in one day?

Do you think that you should be the first to have every new thing that comes out?

Do you get mad when you can't have things your way?

Do you get upset when your friends are late?

Date   /   /

Let's Talk About
LEADERSHIP

Do you know the meaning of the word *leadership*?

Do you think that anybody can become a leader?

Do you think that you can be a leader? Why?

Do you think that leaders are born or made? Why?

Do you think that skin color can determine whether or not someone would be a good leader?

Do you think that gender can determine whether or not someone would be a good leader?

Do you think that you can learn leadership skills?

Do you think that the location where you live can determine whether or not you would be a good leader?

Date   /   /

Let's Talk About
RELATIONSHIPS
Do this exercise with a parent or an adult.

What does the word *relationship* mean to you?

Who can you be in a relationship with?

Do you think that you should need permission from your parents to be in a relationship with anyone?

How old do you think you should be before you get into a relationship?

How long do you think relationships are supposed to last?

If you are in a relationship with one person, are you allowed to see anyone else on the side?

Do you think that it is OK to be in a relationship with more than one person at a time?

Date   /   /

Let's Talk About
WHEN NO MEANS NO
Do this exercise with a parent or an adult.

When does no mean no?

When people tell you that they don't want to have sex, are you supposed to force them to have sex anyway?

If someone tells you to stop trying to have sex with him or her, should you leave him or her alone?

Should you take advantage of people because you are bigger than them?

Should you take advantage of people when they have been drinking alcohol?

Do you think that it is OK to take advantage of someone when they are not in the right state of mind?

Date   /   /

Let's Talk About
SEX

Do this exercise with a parent or an adult.

Do you think that you are ready to have sex?

Do you want to have sex because your friends say that they have had sex?

Do you know what it means to wear protection?

Do you think that you are ready to take care of a baby?

Do you know what venereal diseases are?

Do you know what HIV is?

Do you think that you can die from an HIV infection?

Do you think that you can die from any venereal disease?

Date   /   /

Let's Talk About
TEENAGE PROSTITUTION
Do this exercise with a parent or an adult.

Has an older person ever tried to get you to sell your body for drugs?

Has anyone ever tried to offer you money for selling your body?

Has anyone ever tried to get you to take off your clothes for money?

Do you have any friends who think it is OK to get paid for having sex?

Have adults ever asked you to meet up with one of their friends for money, drugs, or anything else?

Have adults ever promised to give you gifts if you had sex or preformed sexual acts with them or their friends?

Date   /   /

Let's Talk About
DATING

Do this exercise with a parent or an adult.

Why do you think people date each other?

Do you think that a girl is supposed to date another girl?

Do you think that a boy is supposed to date another boy?

Do you think that it is anyone else's business to know whom you are dating?

At what age do you think you should be able to start dating?

Do you know what a chaperone is?

Does dating mean that you are going out together?

Does dating mean that you are more than friends?

Date   /   /

Let's Talk About
FLIRTING

What does the word *flirting* **mean to you?**

Do you ever flirt with the opposite gender?

Do you ever flirt with the same gender?

When someone flirts with you, do you think that they like you?

Would you like your girlfriend to flirt with other guys?

Would you like your boyfriend to flirt with other girls?

Do you think that some flirting is misleading?

Do you think that it is possible to flirt unconsciously?

Do you think that some flirting is really just teasing?

Date   /   /

Let's Talk About

LOVE

Do this exercise with a parent or an adult.

What do you know about love?

Do you think that you are in love?

Do you think that you can be in love with more than one person at a time?

Do you and your friends talk about love?

How can you tell when you are in love?

Do you think that you should be able to love anybody?

Do you think that boys should only be in with love girls?

Do you think that girls should only be in love boys?

Do you think that it's fair to tell someone that you love him or her when you really don't?

Do you think that it's fair to tell someone that you love him or her so that he or she will have sex with you?

Do you think that it's fair to tell people that you love them so that they will buy you things?

Date   /   /

Let's Talk About
CHEATING AND RELATIONSHIPS

Do you think that anyone will ever cheat on you?

Do you think that you will ever cheat on anyone else?

What do you consider to be cheating?

Do you think that everyone should have the option to cheat?

Do you think that people don't know what they are doing when they are cheating?

Is it considered cheating to go out on a date with someone other than your boyfriend or girlfriend?

Is it considered cheating to talk on the phone with an old boyfriend or girlfriend?

Is it considered cheating to stay in touch with an old lover?

Is it considered cheating to text an old or new admirer?

Is it considered cheating to text people or give them your phone number?

Is it considered cheating to give or receive gifts?

Is it considered cheating to flirt with other boys and girls?

Is it considered cheating to touch another person?

Is it considered cheating to go to another person's house?

Date   /   /

Let's Talk About
FEELINGS

Do you keep your true feelings locked up inside until you get to know someone?

Are you afraid to let people know how you really feel?

How often do you express your feelings?

Do people hurt your feelings every day?

Are you mad about something every day?

Do you need to talk to someone about the way that you feel?

How do you feel today?

Whom do you talk to when someone hurts your feelings?

Date   /   /

Let's Talk About
ABUSE

Do this exercise with a parent or an adult.

Are you in any kind of pain today?

Has anyone ever put his or her hands on you?

Have you had any accidents around your house lately?

Do you have any bruises or marks on your body?

Do you miss school because you were recently beaten?

Do you feel scared at home?

Do you sometimes think about running away?

Do you ever think about killing yourself or other people?

Date   /   /

Let's Talk About
MENTAL ABUSE

Do you know what the phrase *mental abuse* means?

Do your friends tease you all the time?

Do your parents always put you down?

Has anyone ever told you that you will never amount to anything when you grow up?

Has anyone ever told you that you are worthless?

Does your boyfriend or girlfriend always put you down?

Has anyone ever told you that they wish that you had never been born?

Date   /   /

Let's Talk About
PHYSICAL ABUSE

Do you know what the phrase *physical abuse* means?

Have you ever wished that someone would stop putting his or her hands on you?

Has anyone ever sexually abused you and you were too afraid to tell anybody about it?

Has anyone ever threatened to hurt you or anyone in your family if you told anyone about him or her sexually abusing you?

Do you ever feel like running away from home?

Are you afraid to go to bed at night?

Date   /   /

Let's Talk About
PEOPLE-PLEASING

Do you know what the phrase *people-pleasing* means?

Do you like to wait on people or do you like to have other people wait on you?

Do you go out of your way to please other people?

Do you want everyone to like you?

Do you cry when people yell at you?

Do you cry when people don't like you?

Do you let people bully you?

Do you let people call you names?

Do you do everything that people tell you to do?

Date   /   /

Let's Talk About
EXPRESSING YOURSELF

How do you express yourself?

What kind of person do you think you are? Why?

Do you think that you are an outgoing person?

Do you like to speak your mind?

Do you keep your feelings locked up inside until you feel like you are going to explode?

Do you just go with the flow? Why?

Do you like to sing?

Do you like to dance?

Do you like to wear nice clothes?

Do you think that you are a materialistic person? Why?

Date   /   /

Let's Talk About
WHAT MAKES YOU MAD

Do you get mad very easily? Why?

Do you get mad when you don't get your way?

Do you get mad when your parents tell you that you can't do something because it's not safe?

Do you get mad when you can't go out with your friends?

Do you get mad when you make mistakes?

Do you get mad when other kids make fun of you?

Do you get mad when you are not allowed to eat what you want to eat?

Date   /   /

Let's Talk About
WHAT MAKES YOU HAPPY

Are you happy when you are doing what you want to be doing?

Are you happy when you are doing what your friends are doing?

Are you happier at your friend's home than you are at your own home? Why?

Do you feel happy when no one is telling you what to do?

Are you happy when you are at home by yourself? Why?

Do you feel happy when your friends share their things with you?

Do you feel happy sharing your things with your friends?

Date   /   /

Let's Talk About
FEELING SAD

When do you feel sad? Why?

Are you sad because someone has hurt you?

Are you sad because you have lost a loved one?

Are you sad because you are doing poorly at school?

Are you sad because you can't have your way?

Are you sad because you dropped your ice cream?

Are you sad because someone was picking on you?

Date / /

Let's Talk About
FEELING TIRED

Do you always feel tired? Why?

Do you take naps after school?

Do you fall asleep in class?

Do you fall asleep on the school bus?

Do you fall asleep when you are standing in line at school?

Do you fall asleep without even knowing it?

Do friends have to wake you up because you are always falling asleep?

Do you fall asleep because you are often awake all night?

Date   /   /

Let's Talk About
ACTING OUT

What does the phrase *acting out* mean to you?

Why do you act out?

Where do you see kids acting out?

Do you act out when you can't have your way?

Do you think that kids act out because they are on drugs?

Do you think that acting out is good or bad? Why?

How does acting out make you feel? Why?

Do you act out because you are mad? Why?

Date   /   /

Let's Talk About
HITTING
Do this exercise with a parent or an adult.

Do other kids hit you without you hitting them back?

Why do you think other kids hit you?

Do you ever ask the other kids why they hit you?

Do you cry when they hit you?

Do they hit you every day?

Where are you when the other kids are hitting you?

Do you tell your mom or dad that kids are hitting you?

How does it make you feel when someone hits you?

Date   /   /

Let's Talk About
FEAR

Can you tell me what the meaning of fear is?

Are you afraid of certain people? Why?

Are you afraid of certain places? Why?

Are you afraid of certain animals? Why?

Are you afraid of the dark? Why?

Are you afraid of high places? Why?

Are you afraid of certain insects and bugs? Why?

Are you afraid of being alone in your room at night? Why?

Are you afraid of anyone in your family? Why?

Date   /   /

FEAR:

F-ALSE

E-VIDENCE

A-PPEARING

R-EAL

Let's Talk About
TRUSTING
Do this exercise with a parent or an adult.

Are you supposed to trust everyone you meet? Why not?

Are you supposed to tell strangers where you live? Why not?

Are you supposed to trust strangers you meet on the street?

Are you supposed to tell strangers your name?

Are you supposed to communicate with strangers on the Internet?

Are you supposed to agree to meet up with someone you meet on the Internet?

Are you supposed to trust friends of friends?

How do you know if you can trust someone?

Can you look at people and tell if they are trustworthy?

Do you feel that you need a reason not to trust someone?

Do you think that you should be able to trust all of the members of your family?

Can you trust everything that everyone tells you?

Do you trust certain people because other people told you that they trust them?

Before you trust what people tell you, do you think that you should ask your mom or dad if it's OK to trust them?

Date   /   /

Let's Talk About
HOW YOU FEEL ABOUT OTHERS

How do you feel about other people?

How do you feel about people who belong to other nationalities?

How do you feel about people who have better things than you?

How do you feel about people who live in better neighborhoods than you?

Why do you think you like some kids better than others?

How do you feel about boys?

How do you feel about girls?

Date   /   /

Let's Talk About
SELFISHNESS

Do you think that you are a selfish person?

Do you share your things with other people?

Do you only share things with people who share their things with you?

Do you only share your things with kids who play with you?

Do you act selfishly toward other people when your friends tell you to?

Why do you think that people act selfishly?

When you are mad, do you let other kids play with your things?

Date   /   /

Let's Talk About
DREAMS

Do you think your dreams can come true?

What kinds of dreams do you have?

Do you think that your dreams are confusing?

Do you wish that your dreams were real?

Do you dream of bad things?

Do you ever have trouble waking up from your dreams?

Are you afraid to go to sleep at night?

Do you sleep with the light on sometimes?

Date   /   /

Let's Talk About
GOOD ROLE MODELS

Who are some good role models in your life?

Do you think that anyone can become a good role model?

Do you think that your mom and dad are good role models?

Do you want to grow up to be a good role model too?

Who do you want to be like when you grow up?

What can you learn from good role models?

Are professional athletes good role models?

Date / /

Let's Talk About
HELPING OUT
Do this exercise with a parent or an adult.

What does the phrase *helping out* mean to you?

Do you only help out when you get paid?

Do you only help out when someone tells you to?

Do you only help people who help you?

Do you only help out when someone is watching you?

Would you help out a friend?

Do you think that you should ever help a stranger look for a lost puppy?

Date   /   /

Let's Talk About
DEPRESSION

Do you think that you are too young to experience depression?

Do you know what depression feels like?

Do you think that you can get help for your depression?

Do you ever feel like killing yourself?

Do you feel tired all the time?

Do you feel tired sometimes but you don't know why?

Do you stay in the house a lot?

Are there times when you don't want to go to school?

Do you feel alone when you are out with your friends?

Do you feel like nobody loves you?

Do you ever just want to be left alone?

Do you ever lose your appetite?

Do you ever feel confused but you don't know why you feel confused?

Do you ever want to hurt yourself?

Do you ever feel like you want to hurt other people?

Do you ever feel like life is not fair?

Do you ever feel that people don't like you?

Date   /   /

Let's Talk About
YOU

Do you like yourself today?

Do you like your nose?

Do you like the way that you look?

Do you like your lips?

Do you like your body?

Do you like your weight?

Do you like your face?

Do you like your voice?

Do you like your gender?

Do you like your hair?

Do you like your ears?

Do you like your height?

Do you like your glasses?

Do you wish that you were in someone else's body?

Do you think that you need plastic surgery? Why?

Date   /   /

Let's Talk About
GRUDGES

Do you know what the word *grudge* means?

Do you think that anyone has a grudge against you? Why?

Do any of your friends have grudges against anyone? Why?

Does anyone hold a grudge against you because of who you are dating?

Does anyone hold a grudge against you because of where you live?

Do you think that people hold grudges against you because of the clothes that you wear?

Date   /   /

Let's Talk About
HATRED

Why do you think people hate each other?

Do you hate anyone? Why?

Do your friends tell you that they hate other people?

Do your friends tell you that you should hate someone because they hate them?

Do you think that some people hate other people for no reason?

Do you think that some people hate because of where your friends live?

Do you think that people sometimes hate other people because of the colors of their clothes?

Date   /   /

Let's Talk About
ANGER

What makes you angry? Why?

Who makes you angry?

Where do you get angry?

Does having to eat your vegetables make you angry?

Do you feel angry all the time? Why?

Are you angry with anyone at your school?

Are you angry with anyone at home?

Are you angry about where you live?

Are you angry with the people you live with?

Are you angry with your mom?

Are you angry with your dad?

Are you angry about anything today? Why?

Date   /   /

Let's Talk About
SELF-CONTROL

Do you have any self-control?

Do you get mad when you can't have your way?

Do you lose your self-control when you are being punished and break your things up?

Do you lose your self-control when someone says that you can't do something your friends are doing?

Are you easily angered?

Do you lose your self-control when someone hits you?

Do you lose your self-control when you make mistakes?

Date   /   /

Let's Talk About
OTHER PEOPLE

Do you think other people like you?

Do you get along with other people?

Do you like playing with other kids?

Do other kids like playing with you?

Do you share your things with your friends?

Do your friends share their things with you?

Do you care about what your friends think about you?

Date / /

Let's Talk About
CHANGE

What does *change* mean to you?

How do you deal with change?

What changes do you not like? Why?

What would you like to change about your life?

How would you choose to change the world?

How would you choose to change your life?

How would you choose to change the lives of your family members?

How would you choose to change your school?

Date   /   /

Let's Talk About
SNITCHING

How do you feel about people who snitch?

What do you think should happen to people who snitch?

Have you ever snitched on anyone before?

Do you think that people realized when they are snitching?

What would it take for you to snitch on someone?

Would you snitch on someone you didn't like?

If your mom or dad told you to snitch on someone, would you do it?

Date   /   /

Let's Talk About
APPRECIATION

Do you know what the word *appreciation* means?

Do you appreciate the things that your mom and dad do for you?

Do you appreciate the things that you have?

Do you appreciate the freedom that you have?

Do you appreciate the opportunities that you have?

Do you appreciate the friends that you have?

Date   /   /

Let's Talk About

SUPPORT GROUPS
Do this exercise with a parent or an adult.

Do you have a support group?

Do you think support groups can help you at school?

Do you think that you can have a support group at home?

Do you think that support groups can help you become a better person?

Do you think that support groups can help you when you get into trouble?

Do you think that support groups can help you make good choices?

Do you think that support groups can help you with your personal problems?

Date   /   /

Let's Talk About
STRESS

Do you know what the word *stress* means?

Do you think that you are too young to have stress in your life?

Do you know where stress comes from?

Do you think you have any stress in your life?

How do you think you should cope with stress?

Do you know how to prevent some of the stress in your life?

Do you know what positive stress is?

Date   /   /

Let's Talk About
FREEDOM

Did you know that freedom means you have the right to vote?

What does the word *freedom* mean to you?

Do you think that all people should be free?

Do you think that freedom means you can do whatever you want to do?

Do you think that you should have to pay for your freedom?

Do you know how your ancestors paid for your freedom?

Are you familiar with any of your ancestors who might have fought for the freedom that you have today?

Date   /   /

Let's Talk About
SLAVERY

Did you know that with slavery people don't have the right to vote?

Do you know what the word *slavery* means?

Did you know that some people still think that slavery is a good thing?

Did you know that slavery still exists today?

Did you know that many women and children today are enslaved in other countries?

Did you know that slavery still exists in some other countries?

Did you know that people in some states in the United States still believe in slavery?

Date   /   /

Let's Talk About
WORKING WITH OTHERS

Do you like working with other people?

Do you like it when other people work with you?

Do you like it when other people tell you what to do?

Do you like working only with certain groups of people?

Do you think that some people are too bossy?

Do you like telling other people what to do?

Do you like having responsibilities?

Do you sometimes feel like other people want you to do all of the work?

Date   /   /

Let's Talk About
PUNISHMENT

Do you think that people should be punished when they are do something bad?

Who do you think should make decisions about your punishment?

Do you think that you are too old to be punished?

What do you think is an appropriate punishment for doing something wrong?

What do you think is an inappropriate punishment for doing something wrong?

How long do you think your punishment should last?

Date   /   /

Let's Talk About

HELP

Do this exercise with a parent or an adult.

What does the word *help* mean to you?

Do you think that people only need help when they are in trouble?

Do you think that people only need help when they make mistakes?

Do you know that it is never too late to ask for help?

Did you know that it is never too early to ask for help?

Do you think that asking for help is silly?

Do you think that you have all of the answers?

Do you think that you are too smart to ask for help?

Are you to you too shy to ask for help?

Do you think that if you ask for help you will look weak?

Are you aware that you can ask for help with everything that you do?

Did you know that asking for help is a one of the smartest things that you could ever do?

Date   /   /

Let's Talk About
GIVING

What does *giving* mean to you?

Do you think that we should give some of the things we have to people who have fewer things than us?

Do you feel good when you give some of your things to other people?

Should we give food to people who don't have any food?

Do you think that we should give clothes to people who don't have any clothes?

Should we expect anything in return when we give things to other people?

Do you think we should give things to people who don't need our help?

Date   /   /

Let's Talk About
AMBITION

What dose the word *ambition* mean?

What things do you want to accomplish within your lifetime?

What do you want to be when you grow up?

What do you want to do to help other people?

What things are important to you?

How do you want to help the planet?

Are there any sports records that you would like to break?

If you could start any company, what kind of company would you want to start?

Date   /   /

Let's Talk About
EXPECTATIONS

What does the word *expectation* mean?

What are your expectations after high school?

What are your expectations for the future?

Do you have any expectations for college?

What are your expectations for starting a career?

What are your expectations about where you want to live?

What are your expectations for being independent?

Date   /   /

Let's Talk About

PROBLEMS

Do this exercise with a parent or an adult.

What does the word *problem* mean to you?

Do you think you are the only one with problems?

Do you think that some of your problems are too big for you to handle? Why?

Do you think you need to talk to someone about your problems?

How do you handle your problems?

Whom do you tell about your problems?

Do you have any problems right now?

Date   /   /

Let's Talk About
SELF-DESTRUCTIVE BEHAVIOR

What does the phrase *self-destructive behavior* mean to you?

Do you do things that are hazardous to your heath and to other people's health?

Do you do things that you know are not good for you?

Do you do self-destructive things because your friends are doing them?

Do you experiment with drugs because somebody told you it would be cool?

Do you do self-destructive things because someone made you mad?

Date   /   /

Let's Talk About
STAYING ABOVE THE INFLUENCE

Do you like to do things just because your friends are doing them?

How do you stay above the influence?

Do you think that staying above the influence means finding new friends?

Do you think that staying above the influence means finding a new boyfriend or a new girlfriend?

Do you think that staying above the influence means having your own mind and not following the crowd?

Do you think that staying above the influence means you might have to find new friends who feel the same way that you feel?

Date   /   /

Let's Talk About
JUST SAYING NO

What are you supposed to just say no to?

Are you supposed to just say no to drugs?

Are you supposed to just say no to cigarettes?

Are you supposed to just say no to skip school?

Are you supposed to just say no when someone ask you to stealing?

Are you supposed to just say no to hanging out with bad people?

Are you supposed to just say no to cheating and lying?

Are you supposed to just say no when ask to do bad things?

Date   /   /

Let's Talk About
DRINKING BEER

Do you like drinking beer?

Do you think that drinking beer is OK?

Do you think that drinking beer is better than drinking liquor?

Do you think that you can get addicted to drinking beer?

Do you think that drinking beer can lead to doing other drugs?

Do you think that you can handle drinking beer?

Do your friends drink beer?

Do you want to drink beer because your friends drink beer?

Date   /   /

Let's Talk About
ILLEGAL DRUGS

What do you know about illegal drugs?

Do you know how many different illegal drugs are out on the streets?

What illegal drugs have you heard about from your friends?

What illegal drugs have you seen people use in front of you?

Do you think that cigarettes are drugs?

Do your friends talk to you about illegal drugs?

Do your friends talk to you about selling illegal drugs?

Date   /   /

Let's Talk About
CIGARETTES

Do you like the smell of cigarettes?

Do you like the way cigarettes make you feel when you smoke them?

Do you like the way people look when they are smoking cigarettes?

Do you think that smoking cigarettes makes you look cool?

Do you want to smoke because your friends smoke?

Do you want to smoke because you think that girls will like it?

Do you want to smoke because you want to be like everyone else?

Date   /   /

Let's Talk About
MARIJUANA

Have you ever smoked marijuana?

How do you get money for the marijuana that you smoke?

Do you lace your marijuana with any other drugs?

Are you addicted to marijuana or any other drugs?

Do you like how marijuana makes you feel?

Does smoking marijuana make you feel grown up?

Do you drink when you smoke marijuana?

Why don't you smoke marijuana?

Do all of your friends smoke marijuana or drink?

Do you think that smoking marijuana can be additive?

Do you smoke marijuana before you go to school in the morning?

Do you think people can't tell when you have been smoking marijuana or drinking beer?

Do you think any of your friends are addicted to marijuana or beer?

Date   /   /

Let's Talk About
PRESCRIPTIONS DRUGS

Do you take prescription drugs?

Do you know what prescription drugs are?

Do you like the way prescription drugs make you feel?

Do your friends like taking pills?

Can you name some prescription drugs that are in your home?

Do you think you should take prescription drugs that have not been prescribed for you?

What do you think would happen to you if the police caught you with prescription drugs that were not yours?

Date   /   /

Let's Talk About
SELLING DRUGS

Have you ever sold any drugs?

Do you think you have to sell drugs to survive?

Do you think that some people have to sell drugs to survive?

Do you think that there are other ways of surviving than selling drugs?

Do you think that it hurts your community to have drugs around?

Where do you think that drugs come from?

How do you think you can help your community with its drug problem?

Date   /   /

Let's Talk About
GAMBLING ADDICTION

Do you like to gamble at school?

Do you like shooting dice with your friends?

Do you like playing card games for money?

Do you gamble until you have no money left?

Do feel like fighting after you have lost all of your money?

Do you want to rob people after you lose all of your money?

Do you try to sell your jewelry or other things after you lose all of your money?

Do you gamble with other people's money?

Date   /   /

Let's Talk About
GUNS

Do you like guns?

Do your friends like guns?

Does your dad have any guns at your home that you are aware of?

Does your dad like to go hunting?

Do you think you would like to go hunting someday?

Have you ever held a gun before?

Have you ever shot a gun before?

Have you ever lost a friend because of a shooting accident?

Do you think that kids should play with guns?

What should you do if you ever find a gun?

What should you do if you see someone at school with a gun?

Have you ever felt like you needed to bring a gun to school?

Do your friends ever talk about shooting anyone?

Do you hear a lot of gunfire where you live?

Date   /   /

Let's Talk About
GANGS

Do you think that gangs are fun?

Do you want to be in a gang? Why? Why not?

What colors do the gang members wear in your neighborhood?

Do you think that gangs are cool? Why? Why not?

Why do you think people want to be in gangs?

Do you think all gang members are bad?

Do you think all gang members do drugs?

Date   /   /

Thoughts

Thoughts

Thoughts

Thoughts

Thoughts

Thoughts

Thoughts

Thoughts

Thoughts

Thoughts

About the Author

Terry Perkins believes in family values. He is a father, a brother, a grandfather, a friend, and a veteran of the U.S. Army. He believes that open communication should be the number one priority in all of our lives. He feels that if we don't express our feelings and opinions shamelessly and in a nonviolent manner, then we are sending a bad message to our children. He hopes that his books will help people communicate openly in their homes, their schools, and their neighborhoods. His goal is to let children know that violence is not the solution for any problem, and he is trying to make a difference one book and one child at a time.